A

Protecting Your Child from Harmful Influences

(Handbook & Journal)

By Carletta D. Washington, Ed. S.

P.O. Box 2535
Florissant, Mo 63033

Copyright ©2010 by Carletta Washington

All Rights reserved. No part of this book may be reproduced or transmitted in any forms by any means, electronic, mechanical, photocopy, recording or otherwise, without the consent of the Publisher, except as provided by USA copyright law.

All Prioritybooks titles are available at special quantity discounts for bulk purchases for sales promotions, premiums, fund-raising, institutional or educational use. For information regarding discounts for bulk purchases, please contact Prioritybooks Publications at 1-314-306-2972 or info@prioritybooks.com. You can contact the author at: education4all@hotmail.com.

Edited by: Lynel Washington and Kendra Koger
Cover Designed by: Sheldon Mitchell of Majaluk
Library of Congress Control Number: 2010925304
ISBN: 978-0-9819913-4-4

First Prioritybooks Printing: April 2010
10 9 8 6 5 4 3 2 1

Printed in the United States of America

Table of Contents

Dedication	3
Foreword	5

Part I
In the Beginning

Chapter 1 Setting the Scene	11
Chapter 2 Moving On	15
Chapter 3 "Mr. Right" Found	19
Chapter 4 Time to Make It Legal	23

Part II
The Big Bad Wolf

Chapter 5 Big Bad Wolf #1: In the Neighborhood	29
Chapter 6 Big Bad Wolf #2: In the Family	35
My Daughter's Biological Father's Family, His Former Sister-in-Law	38
Chapter 7 Big Bad Wolf #3:	

The Opposite Sex 43

Chapter 8
Big Bad Wolf #4:
The Internet Chat Room 47

Chapter 9
Big Bad Wolf #5:
Some of My Child's Friends 53

Chapter 10
Big Bad Wolf #6:
Fashion 57

Part III
You're Invited

Chapter 11
Who Should Be Allowed in the Village? 65

Chapter 12
You're Invited: My Mother 71

Chapter 13
You're Invited: My Uncle and Aunt 75

Chapter 14
You're Invited: My Husband's Parents 81

Chapter 15
You're Invited:
Our Pastor, His Wife, and Our Church Family 85

Chapter 16
You're Invited:
My Child's Teachers, Counselor and Administrators 89

Chapter 17

You're Invited: God and Prayer	93

Part IV
On to a New Beginning:
The Next Phase of Motherhood

Chapter 18 Now that We're "Empty Nesters"...	101
Chapter 19 I Wish for My Daughter...	105
Chapter 20 I Wish for My Family...	109
Chapter 21 She's Back...	115
Chapter 22 The Next Phase of Motherhood...	119
Chapter 23 A Toast to the Happy Times...	123

Part V
Tips for Communication and Support

Communicating with Your Child	130
Signs That Your Child is Going Astray	131
Finding Support in Your Spouse	132
Finding Support in Others	133
Maintaining Your Sanity	134

Basis for Book:
"It takes a village to raise a child."
--African Proverb

Dedication

This book is dedicated to all of the past, present, and soon-to-be mothers. I wish current and future mothers all the best as you come to learn who and what to place in your child's village. If you have a solid family foundation that includes God, a strong work ethic, an appreciation for others—especially the less fortunate—and a vision for you and your family's future, you already have the key ingredients for raising a successful child. So, don't second guess yourself or let others who are contrary make you feel indifferent about your parenting skills. At the other extreme—if your child strays, just know that if the foundation is strong enough, your child's life will eventually come full-circle.

This book is also dedicated to my husband, one of the best "stepfathers" I know! I'm glad we have been able to endure the joys and woes of parenting TOGETHER! Thanks for supporting me in motherhood!

This book is also dedicated to the countless others who helped "raise" my daughter, respecting my husband and me as parents, and guiding us in our decision-making efforts as parents in every stage of our daughter's development as an infant, toddler, child, adolescent, teenager, and now adult! It would have been more difficult without you—especially each time other adults opened their doors and made it easy for our daughter to leave home.

Foreword

You've heard the African proverb, "It takes a village to raise a child." Well, sometimes, some of the wrong people can take up residence in your child's village—with and without your permission. When this happens, be prepared to "fight" not only for—but also—with your child (metaphorically speaking, that is). We had raised our daughter to be very outgoing, respectful, athletic, college-bound, and cautious in her thoughts, words, and deeds. Although there were a few hills and valleys along the way, nothing prepared us for those obstacles that became part of our daughter's "village." Much of the village has remained intact and has been just fine, so I wouldn't question much of our parenting choices. However, like many parents, there are some things that we wish we would have done a little differently in order to avoid the problems we faced.

This book will take you on my personal journey of parenting from single motherhood, to the fairy tale marriage and family, to being an "empty nester." My account is meant to be factual and not an attack on anyone, which is why the names of those involved in not-so-favorable situations have been omitted. However, if you happen to know them or guess who they are, please don't judge them. There is no animosity, just the utmost of precaution when it comes to sharing information that relates to our child and what goes on in our household for fear of potential misguidance and prejudgment on the part of others based on our previous encounters over the years.

This book will also call you to journal your experiences as a mother. Reflection is paramount to understanding who we are as individuals—in this case—mothers. It is so easy to question and doubt our ability to parent, and to measure ourselves as mothers against other matriarchs. However, if we are rooted in God, believe in Christ, and are guided by the Holy Spirit, I strongly believe that we will never fail as mothers—no matter what becomes of our children. Prayer and personal reflection will keep us on track as we prepare for, or continue serving, in our roles as mothers.

This is not a book that will tell you what to do as a mother. It is merely meant to share my experiences. It is also a form of personal healing. I had always hoped that my daughter would remain home until she finished high school and went to college and/or obtained a career that she felt could sustain a decent lifestyle for her. Never in a million years would I have imagined that she would attempt to leave home and then finally do so on bad terms before graduating high school, taking away every moment that moms live for—prom, graduation, college acceptance, etc. and giving those joys and other maternal responsibilities to others, without my approval.

Am I angry with my child? No, just sad and disappointed. But I used to get angry from time-to-time at the adults who were in my daughter's village, taking advantage of her naiveté. I was sometimes livid at the adults in her village who continued to assist her in making poor decisions. I was even often angry at the fact that they had either raised or were raising their own children, but didn't seem to value the fact that my husband and I had never interfered or criticized their parenting either to them or their children, but yet—they felt justified in going behind our backs to help our daughter rebel against us. These same people never attempted to take any steps to bring our family together—only making demands for the care and material welfare of our daughter—even though they had overstepped our authority and boldly invited her into their homes; in reality, they were not willing to fully take responsibility for her. To this, I say they should have SENT OUR DAUGHTER HOME WHERE SHE BELONGED!

Please don't think anger consumed my husband and me. The reality of our situation hit us like a ton of bricks at times. However, with the assistance of prayer, those who had our family's best interest at heart, and other parents who were experiencing the same thing (there are a lot of parents going through this; my problem is not unique), the anger didn't last long. We also realized that we had taught our daughter to think for herself and that she knew right from wrong. So, whether she became a "prodigal" daughter or not wasn't even the issue. We prayed for her salvation and God's protection. We knew that everything else would eventually fall into place, if these two were in order.

Another reason for this book is in hopes of my daughter reading it and better understanding why I made certain decisions as her mother, and that all I want (like many mothers) is for her not to make unwise decisions and to adequately prepare herself for a successful life as an adult. I desire the best God has to offer her and I know that the sky is the limit! He did it for me! I want her to know that she was and is loved by her stepfather and me. If she never reads this book anytime soon, may she read it before she has her first child (whenever that may be) because it may make more sense and be of greater value to her at that time.

I hope that all readers will enjoy this journey through motherhood and find comfort in who they are and the joy God has brought them and their family. Remember to have joy in the good and bad moments. Many are watching you and your actions speak volumes. That is why my husband and I hold no anger against anyone. We know that some parents never get to see their child grow up to accomplish all that we have: accepting Christ at a young age, an A average each year of school, over forty trophies for dance and sports competitions throughout St. Louis and the U.S., obtaining a driver's license, cooking lessons, campaigning for homecoming and class officer, experiencing great health with no major illnesses beyond the chicken pox, no teen pregnancy, and eighteen years of living. These are proof that we did something right! These are the moments God gave us to rejoice in when the world has tried to tear us down and say we were terrible parents! That is why there is no anger, and I can write this book. Someone other than me needs to be reminded of how great of a mother she was, is, and will be. That someone may be YOU!

Part I
In the Beginning

Chapter 1
Setting the Scene

Do you ever wonder why you were exposed to fairy tales, religion, character education, and family values at such a young age? Did you reject some of these traditions? As a mother of a young adult daughter, I now realize, more and more, the importance of these traditions. Let me take you back to the beginning of motherhood for me.

I came from a two-parent, middle-class home in the suburbs. I attended private school, then went to a public high school, and later a state university. I met my daughter's father while in the latter half of high school. We had a somewhat decent relationship at first, but it later became rather rocky and one of those "on and off again" relationships into our first year of college, which is when we became parents. Before the news of us becoming parents, our original plans were to improve our relationship, graduate from college, get married, and travel for at least five years so that we could enjoy each other and life before having any kids. But that's not what happened.

It was scary being pregnant. I knew I wanted the best for my daughter. So, since her father and I seemed to be going nowhere, I decided to focus on completing my Bachelor's degree and taking care of my daughter. This is not to say he wasn't a decent man, he just wasn't in my "fairy tale." Honestly, I knew that from the beginning, but I "hung in there" anyway. I always say that we see the signs early, but we choose to ignore them. Especially as women—we think things will get better or that we can change our man. Then, after we get burned, we talk poorly about the man and sentence him to eternal damnation, simply because the relationship didn't work. My mother always said that just because a man is not with you, doesn't mean that he won't be a great person for someone else! Ladies, let's remember—what you see is what you get. You don't raise men, you raise children.

Reflection Journal

Question: Think back to when you first learned that you were pregnant. How did you feel? What was your circumstance? Was it a fairy tale? If not, what decisions would you like to see your child make so that the news of him or her becoming a parent is a fairy tale moment? _____

_____
_____
_____
_____
_____
_____
_____
_____
_____
_____
_____
_____
_____
_____
_____
_____
_____
_____
_____
_____
_____
_____
_____
_____
_____

REFLECTION JOURNAL

Chapter 2
Moving On

Moving on isn't as easy as it may sound—especially when you have a little one to take care of and you still feel a little something for your child's father. Part of my residual feelings was due to the fact that I had a daughter. I knew there was NO way any man was going to be around her if he couldn't meet my standards! He had to be decent, God-fearing, loving, have a good job or be in college like me, and come from a good family. He had to respect my daughter and me as a complete package. Also, have a car; I had grown up riding the bus for years and after riding the bus with my book bag on one shoulder, a diaper bag on the other, carrying my daughter in her pumpkin seat, and having to walk several blocks to and from home as well as to and from the babysitter's house and across the University of MO-St. Louis' (UMSL) campus and run from one bus stop to another, hoping not to miss my connecting bus—a man with a car was a MUST (Just keepin' it real)!

I knew that choosing not to remain in a relationship with my daughter's father would mean adding more people to her life. This was a struggle for me—especially since I had a few doubts about some of her father's family. So, the thought of adding someone else and his family was somewhat terrifying.

Reflection Journal

Question: During our lifetime, we all have to "move on." Think back to some of the decisions that you have made as a mother that show your ability to successfully "move on." How would you retell this experience to your child in order to help him or her to be able to do the same, either now or in the future?

REFLECTION JOURNAL

REFLECTION JOURNAL

Chapter 3
"Mr. Right" Found

I actually met the man who became my daughter's stepfather and my husband in college prior to my pregnancy. We were only on a "casual" hello and how are you basis, but no real conversation for any length of time. However, after deciding to move on and setting my criteria for the future father to my daughter and my husband, I began to consider this man as part of my fairy tale. So, through a mutual friend, we went on the first of several group dates and had many conversations so that we could get to know one another.

Getting to know each other was important. Plus, I had decided that if a man didn't have the chance to care for my daughter while she was under 4 years of age, I would remain single and he would never meet her. I just didn't want anyone who didn't have the opportunity to raise and discipline my daughter in a loving manner as well as watch her grow up from a toddler into a little girl and into a teenager and young lady. I wanted a man who would actually feel as though she was his own daughter, while respecting the fact that she had a biological father. I also wanted a man whose family could handle the existence of my daughter's biological father in her life as well.

"Mr. Right" was great with my daughter. Everyday after I'd get out of class, he was there to take me to pick her up from the babysitter's home. As she and I came down the stairs to enter the car, he and my daughter would play their own version of "Peek-a-Boo." The two of them would laugh and talk as he drove the two of us home. He also had wonderful parents and a great work ethic; he was "Mr. Right!" Both my daughter and I approved!

Reflection Journal

Question: What qualities did you seek in your "Mr. Right"? How have those qualities benefited your child? _____

REFLECTION JOURNAL

Chapter 4
Time to Make It Legal

I had been living with my "Mr. Right" and his parents for some months after someone broke into my studio apartment. I didn't want to send the wrong message to my daughter who was about three at the time. Also, it didn't help that one of my uncles, who was a deacon at the church we attended, would remind me of the consequences of my living arrangements. Actually, "Mr. Right" and his father worked at night, so we ladies (my mother-in-law, my daughter, and me) had the home to ourselves in the evening. My daughter slept with me in his room. "Mr. Right" would sleep in the family room on the other side of the house. I understood my uncle's point. In addition, I had managed to secure a teaching position after graduating from college and didn't want to stand before my students a pregnant single mother; I felt that would not be a very good example.

Even though these points added pressure on top of pressure, I knew how much "Mr. Right" and his family loved both my daughter and me. There was no question or doubt in my mind as far as my daughter's love for them. Oddly, my daughter's father and his family seemed to approve of my "Mr. Right"—despite thier hopes of her father and me getting back together. Most importantly, I could picture living a "fairy tale" with this "Mr. Right."

Seven months after my husband and I were married, we bought a beautiful home in which to raise our daughter. Now, I had achieved my "fairy tale"—despite the turns I had taken earlier.

REFLECTION JOURNAL

Reflection Journal

Question: Marriage shows a sense of "unity." Why is it important for couples to be on the same page when it comes to parenting? What are some decisions that you feel would be best made by both parents? _____

_____
_____
_____
_____
_____
_____
_____
_____
_____
_____
_____
_____
_____
_____
_____
_____
_____
_____
_____
_____
_____
_____
_____
_____
_____
_____

REFLECTION JOURNAL

REFLECTION JOURNAL

Part II
The Big Bad Wolf

Chapter 5
Big Bad Wolf #1: In the Neighborhood

Fairy tales do come true,
but beware—
there are a lot of big bad wolves lying in Grandma's bed,
waiting to deceive you.

My husband and I did what we could to provide the best environment for our daughter by setting limits, instilling family values, enrolling her in Christian schools, taking her to church and other church-related activities, fostering her musical and dance skills, exposing her to people of varied backgrounds so that she would not want to think she was better than others; teaching her to think about situations critically so that she could make good decisions and surrounding her with family and friends who had her best interest at heart. Of course, when something seems too good to be true, Murphy's Law will kick in and something WILL go wrong!

Our daughter was only four years old when we moved into our home. Because she was so young, we allowed her to play and ride her tricycle only on our block. We were fine until one of our new neighbors moved in, with a son a few years older and a daughter a few years younger than my daughter; the mother felt my daughter should be allowed to ride her tricycle throughout the neighborhood and to play with other children without any restrictions. Immediately, a red flag went up; I felt as if she was questioning my ability to be a good mother. This mother of two also criticized me for enrolling my daughter in dance and various activities because my daughter didn't just "hang out" in the neighborhood as did her children.

My husband and I eventually decided to allow these new neighbors into our daughter's village. However, not without limits! Over the years, I noticed that although this particular mother's little girl was younger than our daughter, she appeared to be a little more advanced than my child. For instance, her mother would allow her to watch movies that included sexual ideas and language—despite parental warnings on the package. Even worse, the mother seemed to have little respect for our rules and expectations. If I expected my daughter to return home at a certain time, the mother would allow my daughter to stay later and then make excuses for her. This really became a concern as the kids grew into adolescence. I was worried about my daughter and her son "getting curious" as some children do in the early stages of development—especially since the family lived in a two-story home and the parents didn't always seem to monitor the children while they were upstairs. Because the father worked nights, he was usually asleep and my daughter would often report that the mother spent time downstairs while the kids played upstairs.

Whenever I'd approach the mother, she was quick to refute my concerns. As my daughter approached adolescence, I learned that my daughter liked her son, so I no longer allowed her to go to their home, but permitted his little sister to visit our home. At times, I even allowed her brother to visit as long as he and the girls were not too far from my view. As time passed, several incidents involving our neighbors made it necessary for my husband and I to attempt to evict them from our daughter's village if we wanted to see her make better decisions. Unfortunately, my husband and I received periodic, late night prank calls and our truck was vandalized. Neighborhoods should be places where parents respect and support each other.

I saw my daughter's village being invaded. She began to speak of running away on a frequent basis. At one point, she mentioned that she wanted to live with the neighbor and her two children. Although the mother was experiencing family problems, she was comfortable with my daughter living with her—even though she now had a teen age son. Fortunately, my daughter's secret desire to leave ended (or so we thought).

REFLECTION JOURNAL

Reflection Journal

Question: Are there influences in your neighborhood that could possibly hinder the success of your child? How is your child's neighborhood different than the one in which you lived as a child? _____

REFLECTION JOURNAL

Chapter 6
Big Bad Wolf #2: In the Family

My In-Law

I speak highly of my mother and father-in-law, but not so much in regard to my sister-in-law. I take objection to the way in which she has interfered with the raising of our daughter. My husband and I were in total disbelief when we learned that she was helping our daughter to communicate with certain individuals, one in particular, as well as view certain television shows and movies, despite our objections. Most upsetting was the fact that my daughter had talked about us and confided in her about running away.

My sister-in-law's actions hurt my family dearly. As a mother, I had expected her to keep me informed about my daughter and what she was experiencing. This would allow us to work together as mothers—and family—to help my daughter be successful in reaching her full potential and obtaining all that God has for her. Unfortunately, monitoring those in your child's village can mean even keeping your family members out.

REFLECTION JOURNAL

Reflection Journal

Question: What values did you learn from your family as you grew up? Which of your spouse's (or significant other's) family members come closest to sharing the values that you want to instill in your child? Have you personally invited these family members into your child's village? _____

REFLECTION JOURNAL

My Daughter's Biological Father's Family, His Former Sister-in-Law

My daughter did eventually leave home. For a time, she had been telling my husband and me that she was going to move in with her aunt on her biological father's side (her father's ex-sister-in-law). (Before I go on, I must let you know that my daughter's father passed away shortly after she turned six years old.) I didn't believe this to be true! My husband and I had heard this threat twice before and certainly the legal age for leaving home was eighteen. Wrong on both accounts! And of course, even though I had tried to maintain contact with my daughter's father's ex-sister-in-law and her three girls, she did not even call me to see if everything was okay. She took my daughter at her word and began to criticize me when I called to verify what my daughter was saying about their relationship and being able to move in with them. One week after Thanksgiving, my daughter went to live with her and her daughters. The drama that developed from this situation grew tumultuous and dragged on until late February, when my daughter returned home.

My Daughter's Biological Father's Family, His Mother

Shortly after my daughter returned home, she left Easter morning before we could make it to church. After moving in with her boyfriend, his sister, and their father for a short while, my daughter eventually moved in with her biological father's mother. Prior to that, although I had a few suspicions where her grandmother was concerned, I had naively continued to encourage a relationship between her and my daughter, particularly after the passing of her son, my daughter's father.

Unfortunately, my daughter living with her grandmother brought trouble as well. Although my daughter left home on her own shortly after turning seventeen, her grandmother tried to demand that my husband and I assist her in providing for our daughter beyond paying for her high school tuition, lunch, and medical needs. Her grandmother did nothing to help bring my daughter any closer to resolving whatever issues she was experiencing. Neither was my daughter any closer to reconciling with my husband and me. In fact, after she moved in with her grandmother, we grew even further apart.

REFLECTION JOURNAL

Reflection Journal

Question: If you are no longer with your child's biological father, what provisions have you (or would you) put into place to help make sure his family is able to enjoy a continuous relationship with your child, without them interfering with your parenting and the new life that you are building for your child?

_____
_____
_____
_____
_____
_____
_____
_____
_____
_____
_____
_____
_____
_____
_____
_____
_____
_____
_____
_____
_____
_____
_____

REFLECTION JOURNAL

Chapter 7
Big Bad Wolf #3: The Opposite Sex

Dating as an adult can be quite an experience. Dating as a teen can be even more of an experience! As mothers, we want the best for our children and pray a "fairy tale" for them, regardless of the choices we made in life. I had hoped that by the time my daughter began "officially" dating (with our permission at age sixteen) she would choose a boy from a family with very few issues. He would be in school (public or private), have at least thought about his future (college, work, military) even if he hadn't quite narrowed it down, and he would not be in trouble with the law.

Why did my straight A daughter with both academic and athletic ability, with aspirations to attend college in order to pursue a visual media career as a VJ (video jockey like on the television show "106 & Park"), from a two-parent, middle class home choose to date someone who was so contrary?!? Although it is not customary to choose a mate for our children in this day and age in the U.S., I did believe that it was important to encourage my daughter to be careful whom she chose to date in order to avoid future concerns.

There is so much physical and emotional abuse that takes place in teen dating relationships today. Teen pregnancy and STD's are ever-increasing. I strongly believed that by my daughter choosing a young man who met the criteria previously mentioned in the beginning of this chapter, she would have fewer negative experiences associated with dating. It is still my desire that my daughter will understand—as I have told her— that though someone is not right for you now, that doesn't mean that later he won't be right for you—if he gets his life together. I feel this way about teen relationships more so than adult relationships because kids do a lot of growing up and adjusting to life. Monitoring your child's dating patterns is a must when reviewing those within your child's village.

Reflection Journal

Question: Do you recall any patterns in your dating habits during your teen and adult years? Healthy dating practices can increase the potential for a healthy marriage in the future. What are some guidelines that you've established for your child regarding dating, his or her treatment of others, and how others treat him or her in the relationship? _____

_____
_____
_____
_____
_____
_____
_____
_____
_____
_____
_____
_____
_____
_____
_____
_____
_____
_____
_____
_____
_____
_____
_____

REFLECTION JOURNAL

Chapter 8
Big Bad Wolf #4: The Internet Chat Room

Internet chat rooms for teens and college students have increasingly becoming the rage. Even elementary children will tell you that they engage in Internet chats. Teens are posting half-naked pictures of themselves, throwing up gang signs, and spreading rumors about each other, which leads to conflict at school and within the neighborhood. Dateline and various news stations have documented these and other dangers of Internet chat rooms regarding teens. This makes it all the more imperative that this "big bad wolf" enters your child's village with very limited access—even at the middle and high school levels.

I noticed my daughter continuously playing "solitaire" on the computer once she entered high school. Solitaire is one of several ways in which teens try to disguise their Internet activity; they minimize the Internet site that you want them to avoid and maximize the one that they feel will be most acceptable to you—their parents. Solitaire may show up quite a bit, along with a MS Word document. My daughter thought I didn't know what she was doing, but I was able to catch her at least once or twice as she tried to switch the screens.

My husband and I decided to "give in" to the Internet chat room craze by discussing with our daughter the dangers of posting too much information as well as the wrong image to those who were able to view her page. However, while we tried to monitor her page, those on her page were not so cautious in their introductions and the pictures they posted on the site. My daughter didn't appear to give much thought to the phrase "being known by the company you keep." Then again, how many teens do? This is evident by the postings on the chat room pages. We noticed teens half-dressed, exposing their chest, pelvis, posing with 40oz beer bottles, blowing kisses in the mirror, and even more! We also noticed that some of the girls called themselves, "B****," "Ho," and even more derogatory names. Kids were also throwing up gang signs and talking about sex; spreading rumors about each other, and giving out personal information such as their real name, school, age, address, where they worked, and posting pictures of their baby siblings.

Eventually, we tried to "shut down" the chat room (at least in our home, anyway) due to the site pages of the "friends" connected to her page and her insistence to continue connecting to boys—one in particular. Of course this caused problems in our household. We knew that she was using the site at her friends' homes, although she knew that this was not something of which we approved. Unfortunately, Internet chat rooms can become rather "addictive" and kids are an easy target! Their naiveté about the "unknown" and eagerness to trust "everyone," except their parents' experience and/or wisdom, makes them a prime target for Internet stalkers as well as Internet abuse.

In the previous paragraph, the term "friends" is written in quotations, because I truly dislike this term when it comes to Internet chat rooms. Friends are people who truly know you and look out for your best interest and the interest of those around you. They respect and care about you, what you stand for, and your family. They don't allow you to bring harm to yourself or others. They are objective when offering their support. (More specific definitions can be found in any standard dictionary, collegiate or student format.) My point is that calling strangers "friends" causes kids to "let their guard down." Perhaps, if they were called, "associates" or some term other than "friends," kids wouldn't be so quickly inclined to tell and show so much. Or, maybe it's the thought of never really ever getting the opportunity to meet any of those with whom they share information that draws children. Either way, the information kids share and behavior in which they engage on the Internet is appalling in many cases.

Reflection Journal

Question: Privacy is a great thing. And, we can't know everything our child is doing. BUT—there is NO excuse for NOT knowing ANYTHING about our child BEYOND what he or she shows us of him or herself. Even when you think you know everything—you find something new—EVENTUALLY. When was the last time you checked your child's Internet History & personal pages (i.e., Facebook, MySpace, Bebo), I-pod, CD & DVD collection, photos, cell phone & cell phone bill, closets, drawers, under the bed, book bag, purse, car, and locker? What are some things you would like to learn about your child's personal life in order to either help you form a closer bond with him or her, or to help him or her to be more successful? _____

_____
_____
_____
_____
_____
_____
_____
_____
_____
_____
_____
_____
_____
_____
_____
_____
_____
_____
_____

REFLECTION JOURNAL

Chapter 9
Big Bad Wolf #5: Some of My Child's Friends

Overall, the friends in my daughter's life have been wonderful! Many of them are from homes such as ours, in which parents want the best and believe in setting limits so that their girls don't grow up too quickly and that they get the best life has to offer. These are the friends who have given her sound advice and attended many of our family's events. These are the friends whose parents have shared their concerns about childrearing and helped us work through some of our toughest parenting issues.

Adults know that you only have one or two really close friends in your lifetime. Kids don't seem to grasp this concept. Earlier, I mentioned some of the "friends" that I had to ban from my daughter's village. Well, there were others such as the one who introduced my daughter to the boy who is so opposite of everything that we have taught her. You know the saying, "Friends don't let friends drink and drive"? Too bad friends don't always help friends make the best decisions about dating, like the one who introduced my daughter to the boy of whom she knew her mother wouldn't approve. Or, like the friends who assisted her in getting messages back and forth on Internet chat rooms to various people—including the guy of whom we disapprove. Or, the friends who loaned my daughter their cell phone and/or mobile SIM/phone card so that she could make phone calls to people without our knowledge—despite the fact that she had virtually unlimited phone privileges.

REFLECTION JOURNAL

Reflection Journal

Question: List the names (legal and nick/street names), phone numbers (cell and home), addresses, schools, and parents (include parents' occupations) of at least five of your child's circle of friends? In the event of an emergency, this may prove to be helpful. _____

REFLECTION JOURNAL

Chapter 10
Big Bad Wolf #6: Fashion

Some of you may be asking: "Fashion?" It's true! Now, we know that each generation has its own fashion craze. Some are good, and some. . .well (smile). I won't deny that I went through the tomboy stage. I felt self-conscious about my "early" and somewhat "noticeable" development. So, I wore baggy pants and large shirts. To draw even less attention to myself, I wore a baseball cap with my hair tucked under, in a ponytail, or just plain ole straight. I didn't want to be a "boy"! I wanted to be noticed, just not for my chest! This stage lasted from late elementary through early middle school.

Then, there was the preppy stage. I wore a matching belt, socks, underwear, and shirt. My shirts were polo and oxfords; I rarely wore jeans, sweats, or tennis shoes. I was more comfortable with my figure, but still wanted to keep a somewhat "low" profile. This stage lasted from late middle school until early high school.

My next phase was the punk rock phase. I liked Cindy Lauper's bushy hair and head bands/scarves (minus the hair cut and color). I also liked her long colorful skirts. I really wanted to be seen! Boy, did I stand out! This was a fun stage for me! This stage was during a small part of my sophomore year of high school.

By the end of high school and into the beginning of college, I adopted a more professional style of dress. I loved eye shadow, eyeliner, lipstick, and nail polish! My goal was to emulate my mother's style of dress! My mother was a secretary. She wore beautiful suits and dresses, and, had a TON of shoes! My mom ALWAYS looked GREAT each morning! Diahann Carroll as Julia and Phylicia Rashad as Clair Huxtable looked as good as her! No one else could compare to my mother! Though I have had a mix of styles since growing up and into adulthood, my professional dress is what I treasure most, because it is a tribute to my mother!

So, where am I going with this you may ask? Well, although fashion didn't cause a problem in my parents' household while I was growing up—particularly because I never went overboard—it did become a problem in my household with my own daughter. Sadly, my refusal to allow her to wear jeans to her paternal grandmother's church on Easter Sunday resulted in my daughter's departure from home. My husband and I eventually learned that she had moved in with her boyfriend, his sister, and their father. A few weeks later, my daughter went to live with her paternal grandmother. Prior to this incident, my husband and I had managed to successfully deal with fashion trends such as fake nails, midriff tops (as long as they stopped at her waist), spaghetti straps, high heel shoes (no stilettos), two-piece swimming suits (as long as they were not too revealing), and hair dye and high lights until an age we felt most appropriate for our daughter. We were fortunate that the storms of short shorts, hi-cut swimming suits, plunging necklines, and other more-adult fashion trends had passed over our home.

Most fashions came in stages or as my daughter grew older. It was difficult for my daughter to see girls younger than her wearing some of the clothes and fashion that I had restricted or forbidden her to wear. By the same token, it wasn't easy trying to teach my daughter to be comfortable with the person she was at each stage of her life. How do you teach your daughter that you don't want her to remain a little girl or to even look like one, you just don't want her looking older than she is at any given moment. Media images make it difficult. Parents who give into the images that are presented to their daughters make it tricky. However, for the mothers who are experiencing the fashion storm—please know that it won't last forever. Fashion is every bit as much about teaching your daughter to love and care for herself as it is about protecting her image and reputation. Compromise where and when you can, and give in only when it's time.

Reflection Journal:

Question: What are some of the stages of fashion that you experienced as a child? In retrospect, what would you change and why? What stages have you experienced with your child? How have you handled these phases? What is it that you want your child's fashion sense to say about him/her as an individual and as a young man/young lady? _____

_____
_____
_____
_____
_____
_____
_____
_____
_____
_____
_____
_____
_____
_____
_____
_____
_____
_____
_____
_____
_____
_____
_____
_____

REFLECTION JOURNAL

Part III
You're Invited

Chapter 11
Who Should Be Allowed in the Village?

You've heard it said that if you want to be successful, you must surround yourself with successful people. Anyone who was willing to help us become successful parents and our daughter to become a successful young lady was permitted into the village. When our daughter was very young, some of the additional people from which she was directed to seek advice included: my mother, my aunts and uncles, my husband's parents, and our pastor. I wanted her to speak to these individuals because I felt they were supportive of us and they had parenting styles similar to my husband and me. I also felt that because most of them had known us from a very young age, they could help my daughter understand why my husband and I made certain decisions. Finally, if necessary, they could help mediate certain situations if my daughter ever felt she couldn't talk to us as her parents.

REFLECTION JOURNAL

Assessment Questions for Considering Members of Your Child's Village

- Individual's name _____

- Relationship to you _____

- Where/When did you meet _____
  _____

- Years of acquaintance _____

- What are the qualities that you admire in this individual that you would like for him/her to share with your child? _
  _____
  _____
  _____
  _____
  _____
  _____
  _____

- How will these qualities benefit you and your child's relationship? _____
  _____
  _____
  _____
  _____

REFLECTION JOURNAL

- In what way has this individual proven to be genuinely supportive of your child-rearing efforts? _____

- In your observation of your child with this individual, how comfortable would you say your child is while in this individual's presence? _____

- In your observation of this individual with your child, how comfortable would you say he/she is while in the presence of your child? _____

REFLECTION JOURNAL

_____
_____

- In your observation of this individual's overall lifestyle (spiritual, personal, professional, financial), how comfortable would you be leaving your child in this individual's care, on a day-to-day basis or in the event that anything should happen to you? _____
_____
_____
_____
_____
_____
_____

- How well would you say that you know this individual? ____
_____
_____
_____
_____
_____
_____
_____

- Is there anything else you'd like to know about his individual? If so, what and why? _____
_____
_____
_____
_____

REFLECTION JOURNAL

- Do you feel this individual would hide anything from you with regard to your child? If so, what, under what circumstances, and why?

Chapter 12
You're Invited: My Mother

Every daughter should be close to her mother; especially as she grows up and has more life experiences. Although I never really felt very close to my mother, I felt deep down inside that she loved me because of all the things she had done for me.

Because I wanted my daughter to be close to my mother, I did my best to foster a relationship between the two of them. I encouraged my daughter to call my mother, to send her birthday cards, and to invite her to her birthday parties each year; we also visited my mother and went to the movies from time-to-time. I did not mind if my daughter contacted my mother for anything—even if she and I disagreed with each other and she wanted to have someone to talk to about our disagreement, because my mother would be able to teach her more about me and why I make certain decisions. My mother would also be able to help mediate any situation objectively, if necessary. I truly believe that mothers know their children—especially their daughters. As females, we share many of the same fears and desires. We are faced with many of the same media images. We experience the same physical changes and challenges. Although our experiences take place at varying degrees, in different time periods, under unique circumstances, mother-daughter experiences are still very similar.

Although my mother and I have had our differences, I have maintained a great deal of respect and love for her over the years. I recall my pride as my mom received compliments from others about her beauty and professional style of dress. I remember her love for grammar, as well as the written and spoken word as she left notes for my siblings and me to do various chores or as she enjoyed getting our brains going with her usual "word of the day." I also remember her strength in the midst of her weakest moments. I have continued to admire and mimic my mother's beauty and inner grace. Today, when people compliment my style, I tell them it's a tribute to my mom.

My mom has always been pretty good about respecting the way in which my husband and I raise our daughter. Sometimes, my relationship with my mom helps to fill the void in my relationship with my daughter. One can never know how their children will feel about them, but it is important to foster a multi-generational relationship between your parents, your children, and yourself. The idea of the past (your parents), present (you), and future (your children) connecting and interacting on a regular basis can be a key element in your child's village.

REFLECTION JOURNAL

Reflection Journal

Question: What makes you smile most when you think of your relationship with your mother, father, or the person who raised you? How does your relationship with your child(ren) compare to that of you and your parent(s)/guardian(s)? _____

_____
_____
_____
_____
_____
_____
_____
_____
_____
_____
_____
_____
_____
_____
_____
_____
_____
_____
_____
_____
_____
_____
_____
_____
_____

REFLECTION JOURNAL

Chapter 13
You're Invited: My Uncle and Aunt

One of my mother's sisters and her husband have been a strong spiritual force in my life for a very long time. Even though I felt that what I told my aunt (during my childhood) would be reported to my mom shortly after I told her, I didn't mind because I had secretly dubbed my aunt as my "mouthpiece" and the "go-between" for my mother and me.

Most importantly, I knew that my aunt and uncle would pray for me, my family, and my friends. Although my faith wasn't very strong while I was growing up, I ALWAYS knew that if I needed help sharing my faith with someone, I could invite them to my aunt and uncle's home for good, clean family fun, delicious food, and prayer. Introducing my friends (and boyfriends) to my aunt and uncle meant a lot to me because they would give me their opinion and help me to establish guidelines for my friends to help ensure their respect for my family and my beliefs.

What I liked most about my aunt and uncle is the fact that they were—in my opinion—the best representation of the ideal family. Their marriage seemed to be strong and stable. They always seemed to be on the same page when it came to taking care of their children and they extended that same love and support to all of their nieces and nephews! I always felt that they wanted the best for me and they had dreams of me being successful in life just as they had dreamed for their own children. My aunt and uncle also had a clearly defined belief system; God and family were always important to them and they never passed up a moment to share their belief in God with people or to welcome others to their home. Finally, I always knew that my parents—especially my mom—approved of my aunt and uncle, because they knew they would help to keep me on the "right" path.

Reflection Journal

Question: Think back to your youth. How did the beliefs and traditions of extended family members align to those of your parents?

REFLECTION JOURNAL

REFLECTION JOURNAL

Chapter 14
You're Invited: My Husband's Parents

I truly believe that when you marry your spouse, you are marrying his parents as well. The relationship you build with other members of his family (i.e., siblings, aunts, grandparents) depends on his relationship with them. Ladies—PLEASE MAKE SURE YOU CAN GET ALONG WITH YOUR MOTHER-IN-LAW!!! You never want to come between your spouse and his parents, or ask him to choose sides. For women, having a strong, objective matriarch is key to helping us grow as a wife in meeting our husband's needs. Although you may have this in your own mother, it never hurts to have additional support from another experienced woman's wisdom and strength to help guide you through marriage. Besides, who better to assist with understanding your husband than the ones who know him best—his parents?

My in-laws' home has been like a second home for over fifteen years; it's where I find peace and comfort. My in-laws are truly supportive of not just their son, but me as well! In addition, because of their love and support for the two of us, they have gone above and beyond to support us as parents in raising my daughter. I have been able to trust them with her. They have treated my daughter as if she was their own biological granddaughter. That is why I love them so much!

Reflection Journal

Question: What do you admire most about your in-laws that make you most comfortable with them spending time with your child(ren)? If you have never felt very close to them, how do you think you can make your relationship with them more comfortable so that your children are not adversely affected? __

REFLECTION JOURNAL

Chapter 15
You're Invited:
Our Pastor, His Wife, and Our Church Family

God should be at the head of every home! To help make this possible is the good teaching of a strong pastor! In our case, we have been blessed with a strong pastor who has a beautiful family that includes his loving wife, who is equally strong and active within the community. Most importantly, they are parents. So, they know what it was like to raise a teen, and having to ward off the dangers awaiting today's youth.

During the tough times that my husband and I experienced with our daughter, we were able to turn to both our pastor and his wife as needed! More specifically, there were times when we needed to speak to both our pastor and his wife; then, there were times when we needed just our pastor. However, the most memorable time for me was when I called my pastor's wife to meet me with my daughter. I needed another God-fearing mother who would be there for me, and, she was there! I was able to talk, cry, hug, and receive counsel and prayer; and to speak to another mother in the midst of my crisis! That night, I received confirmation of my ability as a mother to overcome all that was coming at me in a negative way.

It has meant so much to me to have the support of my pastor and his wife; they have been able to help others better understand our experience. Because of my pastor and his wife's support, we have gained comfort from other parents within our church! We are grateful for their prayers, advice, and support!

Reflection Journal

Question: What are some of the issues facing your family? When it comes to raising your child(ren), what support would you like from your pastor, his wife, and your church family? ____

REFLECTION JOURNAL

Chapter 16
You're Invited:
My Child's Teachers, Counselor and Administrators

As parents, it can be difficult to open up to others for fear of them thinking the "worst" of us—especially when it comes to our child's school! As an educator, keeping my daughter's school informed of various events in her early years was not such an issue, but keeping her school informed of what was going on during her last two years of high school was not only difficult—but embarrassing! Where would I start? I wasn't exactly sure where this turn of events had actually begun.

Well, moms, I am here to tell you that my decision to speak openly and honestly with my daughter's teachers, counselor, and administrators about our family's situation was one of the BEST decisions that I could have made!!! I felt so relieved because my daughter's school really looked out for her and me. They implemented the right amount of empathy and "tough love" at every turn! They also continued to keep me informed and supported my husband and me as our daughter's parents. The support extended to our family from her school was phenomenal!!!

Reflection Journal

Question: What support does your child's school offer parents? Are there any additional support systems that you feel your child's school should include in its programming for parents? What are the specific details/components of the support system(s) that you would like to propose? Complete the proposal outline below and use it as a guide to present your school's parent liaison, parent group, counselor, or administrator.

Parent Support/Program Proposal

Presented by _____

Presented to _____

Date _____

Parent Support/Program Proposal Title _____
_____

Age group/demographics of parents to be served by program __
_____

Meeting Dates/Times _____
_____
_____

Support/Program Goals

#1. _____
_____
_____
_____
_____
_____

REFLECTION JOURNAL

#2. _____
_____
_____
_____
_____
_____

#3. _____
_____
_____
_____
_____
_____

Materials/Resources (i.e., guest speakers, Internet, books, refreshments, money); how often are the materials/resources needed? How much is needed? Who is/are the contact personnel?
_____
_____
_____
_____
_____
_____
_____

The following will be used to evaluate the program to determine its effectiveness: _____
_____
_____
_____
_____

REFLECTION JOURNAL

Chapter 17
You're Invited: God and Prayer

Hmmmm, God and prayer! I cannot say enough about the importance of inviting God and prayer into one's life! Trials and tribulations should encourage us to run all the more diligently toward God and prayer!!! As a result, our trust and faith should increase even more!!! Instead, some of us give up, become angry, make excuses, become depressed, or look for others to blame. These options were available to me and I "dabbled" in them all, but I quickly realized that I had a lot for which to be thankful!

My thankfulness led me to continue reading my Bible each night before going to bed. My thankfulness led me to pray throughout the day for my daughter, the adults and those who had been the "big bad wolf" in our lives, and the future of my family. My thankfulness resulted in an inner peace and assurance in God's promise to take care of my needs and to give me the desires of my heart!!! My thankfulness allowed me to pray without bitterness, anger, confusion, excuses, depression, and blame.

God and prayer also brought my husband and me even closer together!!! It helps to have a spouse to lean on during tough times. Together, my husband and I were able to maintain our strength. Together, we were able to help each other maintain perspective and view each part of our family's situation rationally. We helped each other "face the world head-on!" We looked to each other for support and began to spend more time with one another and continued to attend Church on a weekly basis! That's what God and prayer did for us!!! Our lives never "missed a beat" and most importantly—we kept our sanity!!!

REFLECTION JOURNAL

Reflection Journal

Question:

When and how often do you pray? _____
_____
_____
_____
_____
_____
_____
_____

Are you comfortable praying, or do you prefer others to take the lead in praying? _____
_____
_____
_____
_____
_____
_____
_____
_____

What types of requests/petitions do you include in your prayers? _____
_____
_____
_____

REFLECTION JOURNAL

Describe 1-2 of your prayers that have been answered. ____

REFLECTION JOURNAL

Take time to list 1-2 prayer requests for each of the members of your family. Be specific.

REFLECTION JOURNAL

REFLECTION JOURNAL

Part IV
On to a New Beginning:
The Next Phase of Motherhood

Chapter 18
Now that We're "Empty Nesters"...

Throughout this book, I have either mentioned or implied that our daughter left home. So, moms, I am here to tell you that being an "empty nester" is NOT the end of the world! When our daughter entered high school, some of my friends asked me how I was adjusting to the fact that my daughter would soon be leaving for college or be on her own. My response was simply that we have never raised her to stay at home and that we wanted her to be free to live anywhere she pleased.

While the odds of our daughter eventually leaving the state seemed inevitable, we never figured she'd leave our home sooner than expected! My husband and I have been empty nesters for quite some time now. However, I must confess that for several months after my daughter's last departure, I had left her room just as she left it—in disarray—secretly hoping she would come back home—even if it was only to get her belongings.

Well, it became evident as time passed that I could either keep things as they were, or make a few changes. So, I encouraged my husband to make some MAJOR changes! My cousin, who's a professional painter, painted each bedroom; and through a referral from a couple at church, we were able have the carpet on the main level changed to hardwood floors. To top it all off, we packed our daughter's belongings and delivered them to her paternal grandmother's house, her last known address. Dropping her things off at her grandmother's house came with threats of a restraining order and a hostile visit to our church. But, life goes on!

Because my daughter and I came as a "package deal," my husband and I find ourselves walking down memory lane as certain situations remind us of our daughter and our favorite family moments. However, the freedom for my husband and me to enjoy each other as a couple is both new and very exciting! We recently celebrated fifteen years of marriage and are looking forward to many happy years of continuing to get to know each other, continuing to support each other's dreams, and enjoying our future together! My advice to empty nesters or those who are about to become empty nesters is:

First, know that as long as you have worked to provide your children with a solid foundation, they will be just fine!

Secondly, once your children leave home, they are adults and they have to write their own life story. They are accountable for their own actions.

Finally, from one mother to another, this is your time to "return to self", the "you" whom you may have left behind when your children arrived.

I've lost ten pounds, written this book, and will be completing my dissertation very shortly!!! For me, I am now on to a new beginning: the next phase of motherhood!!!

A MOTHER'S REFLECTION

Reflection Journal

Question: When you become an empty nester, what will you look forward to most and why?

REFLECTION JOURNAL

Chapter 19
I Wish for My Daughter...

My wish for my daughter's future is like any mother's. I wish for my daughter that she seeks God and His wisdom in every circumstance. I wish for my daughter to have ALL of her heart's desires. I wish for my daughter to find her place in this world so that she is successful. I wish for my daughter to find her God-fearing "Romeo" (like I did), get married, and have a beautiful family. I wish for my daughter to have perfect health and a sound mind so that one day, when she becomes a mother, she recalls her fondest memories of growing up and bases the decisions she makes regarding her family in part on the foundation she received in her childhood. I wish for my daughter to now allow me to parent her from the perspective of a mother to a "young adult lady" so that she will realize that I have ALWAYS had her best interest at heart. I wish for my daughter all that I never had, currently have, and hope to have one day. I wish for my daughter that she NEVER chooses the easy way out and NEVER gives up on life, God, her family, or herself.

I have always loved bragging about my daughter and her many accomplishments while she was living at home! I was really proud of her and even more grateful to God for ALL his many blessings! Despite everything, I still ONLY wish the BEST for my daughter. When you give birth to your child, how can you wish for any less—especially as a mother? Each night, I share with God my wishes for my daughter.

REFLECTION JOURNAL

Reflection Journal

Question: What do you wish for your children and their future? Be specific.

REFLECTION JOURNAL

Chapter 20
I Wish for My Family...

I wish for my family what every mother wishes for her family. I wish for my family's peace. I wish for my family's happiness. I wish for my family's togetherness. I wish for my family's simplicity. I wish for my family's spiritual health. I wish for my family's financial health. I wish for my family's physical health. I wish for my family's forgiveness. I wish for my family to have a successful future. I wish for my family's strength. I wish for my family lasting, fulfilling friendships.

Regardless of how you lose a family member (i.e., military, college, marriage, runaway, abduction, divorce, death), your family never returns to its original "family" state. When our daughter left home during high school, my husband and I suffered a great loss. Besides the embarrassment and hurt, we had to deal with the "emptiness" within our home and our hearts.

As a mother, who had brought a child into my husband's life, I felt a sense of guilt. My husband had cared for my daughter unconditionally as if she were his own. After my daughter's father died, my husband really "stepped up to the plate!" I often found it hard to fathom a closer father-daughter pair. They loved most of the same music, the same movies, and they were familiar with the latest shoes and athletic wear. They loved to work out and stay in shape. They loved sports and had a strong interest in mathematics.

My guilt was due to the fact that I had watched him help take care of my daughter without question or demand for a little over twelve years. He never looked for anything in return. He was the perfect role model. How could I begin to fill the void in his life? As time went on, the answer became simple, "just be there for him and focus on building your marriage so that it is stronger than ever." That's exactly what I have set out to do. My husband and I have become even closer and our fifteenth year anniversary was a beautiful testament of that!

As a mother, I felt a gigantic void in my own life. After all, if my daughter left home early, what did that say about my skills as a mother? How could I remain in education, if my own daughter chose to leave home? How could I even continue to want to pursue a career in speaking about parenting? How could I even attend children's events?

I recall attending a basketball game at my daughter's former elementary & middle school and feeling like the game and atmosphere was surreal. I felt so displaced that I asked my husband if we could leave early. A few of my most empty moments included not feeling like I was entitled to celebrate Mother's Day. Another was not being able to continue the tradition of hosting our annual celebration of my daughter's birthday from ages sixteen to eighteen. Each year, since my daughter's birth I hosted an annual birthday celebration in honor of my daughter and invited our family and friends because I was so proud of her and where she and I had come since being a single parent family! That was my way of celebrating my inner joy and peace with having decided to keep my daughter instead of giving her up for adoption.

Another major void was my daughter's senior year of high school. This was the year that I had looked forward to more than almost any other moment of my daughter's life. Every parent looks forward to his/her children graduating from high school. If you can get them through high school without them having any children of their own and/or the interference of drugs and alcohol—you really feel like you've done your job as a parent!

Nevertheless, throughout all that we have experienced, I still wish for my family and all my previous wishes!!! I also wish for my family's ability to continue to hold onto the most fondest of family memories, so that we never lose sight of what matters most next to God—family.

Reflection Journal

Question: What do you wish most for your family? _____

REFLECTION JOURNAL

Chapter 21
She's Back...

My daughter left a few days after high school graduation to be with her boyfriend, who had moved to another state to stay with his sister and their mother. Periodically, our daughter would contact us or leave a message, never failing to mention how well things were going for her. However, my husband and I felt this was not the case.

In October, I began to pray that God give me a sign as to when I should call my daughter to ask her to return to St. Louis. One night, while visiting with my in-laws, my father-in-law told me that he had a feeling that my daughter would return home before the end of he year. This was the second time he had made that prediction. That night, I decided to call her. That's when I learned that all was not well. My daughter had not been living in the best of conditions and was facing financial hardship.

After a very serious conversation with my daughter, I asked her if she would like for us to pay for her to come home. After receiving a firm "yes," my husband and I made arrangements so that she could return by the end of the week. That was the best conversation that I had with my daughter in years! It allowed me the opportunity to be her "mom," guiding and caring for my daughter again!

Since she has been back, our relationship has grown even stronger than before. My daughter is approaching nineteen years old, and I have really enjoyed our time together over the last few weeks!!! As a result, I have been able to enter into the next phase of motherhood, now that she is an adult. There is no more checking up on her, inquiring about her whereabouts, monitoring her activities. I have not even said, "I told you so" to my daughter, and I don't intend to. She has already expressed that she has "messed up."

Right now, I just want to continue to guide her, talk with her, hug her, and spend time together. Even though she hasn't told me everything, she has expressed that she wants to leave again in the very near future. However, she knows that if she goes back, my hope is for her to be more emotionally and financially stable. After all, she's an adult and "the law" tied my hands when she turned seventeen. No, I'm not intending to paint a bleak, grim, or cynical picture—I'm just sharing how as a mother—I have managed to cope with what happened to my family.

Unfortunately, this turn of events still affects my family today. Nevertheless, God has answered my prayer in time for the holidays: my daughter's back, my daughter and I are getting closer, and my daughter and I are on to a new beginning as I experience the next phase of motherhood!!!!!!

Reflection Journal

Question: This section is being completed on the eve of Thanksgiving Day. I am sooo thankful for ALL that God has done to bring my family and me through this situation!!! Please take a few moments to list what you are most thankful for with regard to you and your child's relationship.

_____
_____
_____
_____
_____
_____
_____
_____
_____
_____
_____
_____
_____
_____
_____
_____
_____
_____
_____
_____
_____
_____
_____

REFLECTION JOURNAL

Chapter 22
The Next Phase of Motherhood...

My next phase of motherhood is just beginning!!! I am very excited and fully welcome this new journey!!! As I reflect on my life experience, I think about the many lessons I have learned and how strong I have grown as a Christian, woman, wife, and mother. At first, I questioned how this could have happened to my daughter and me. Now, I realize that I am not the first mother to experience this loss and I won't be the last. Therefore, my goal in writing this book was not to blame anyone, influence legislation, or gain sympathy, I just want to help other mothers in a similar situation by letting them know:

(1) You are not alone. The more you share your story with other mothers, the more information and support you gain.

***

(2) There is hope. Your story is your story and you can influence the outcome based on your actions.

***

(3) With the right individuals involved in your child's village, your bond with your child will remain strong.

***

(4) You can make it through the anger, hurt, and emptiness—if you determine to continue to live without letting them consume you. God knows how much you can bear.

***

REFLECTION JOURNAL

Reflection Journal

Question: Now, you didn't think I was going to get the last word, did you? Please take a few moments to reflect on the lessons you will take from the information in this book. When you have finished, please spend time reading your previous Reflection Journals and begin to apply the information as needed to your life and share your story with another mother. _____

_____
_____
_____
_____
_____
_____
_____
_____
_____
_____
_____
_____
_____
_____
_____
_____
_____
_____
_____
_____
_____
_____
_____
_____

REFLECTION JOURNAL

Chapter 23
A Toast to the Happy Times...

My daughter has decided to leave again in a few weeks. Although it saddens me that she is making this decision, I can at least say that we have made some progress in our relationship since she first left home. Most importantly, I will always hold firm to the memories of the happy times that I have shared with my daughter. Although I don't drink, I'd like to make a toast to the happy times. Here's to...

- The day I learned that I was pregnant with a little girl
- The day my daughter was born
- The day my daughter said her first words
- The day my daughter took her first steps
- The day my daughter began pre-school
- The day my daughter graduated from pre-school
- The day my daughter began kindergarten
- The day my daughter graduated from kindergarten
- The day my daughter was baptized
- The day my daughter graduated from 8th grade
- The day my daughter began high school
- The day my daughter began her 1st job
- The day my daughter learned to drive
- The day I gave my car to my daughter

- The day my daughter was inducted into the National Honor Society
- My daughter's dance and voice lessons, competitions, and recitals
- My daughter learning to ride a bike
- My daughter's basketball and track practices, games, competitions, and tournaments
- My daughter's beauty pageants
- My daughter's school dances and parties
- My daughter's first birthday party
- My daughter's report cards and the completion of class projects
- My daughter's first prom
- My daughter and I singing in the car together
- My daughter and I going shopping and running errands
- Making hot tea to help my daughter feel better
- My daughter and I planning meals from cookbooks and recipes
- Meeting my daughter's friends and their parents
- Seeing my daughter's smile
- Hearing my daughter laughing uncontrollably at I Love Lucy episodes
- Sharing personal stories and talking about deep issues with

my daughter (i.e., boys and music)

- My daughter and I walking the dog together
- My daughter enjoying family vacations
- My daughter and I enjoying our visits to the beauty shop, nail salon, and spa
- Preparing the house for my daughter's sleepovers
- Seeing my daughter's name listed in her high school's alumni book as a recent graduate
- The not-so-happy times, though unfortunate, they have made my daughter and me stronger as individuals, brought me closer to my husband, helped me grow closer to God, and permitted time for me to focus on myself and my needs

REFLECTION JOURNAL

Reflection Journal

Question: Now that you have reviewed your previous journal entries and discussed what you have learned on this journey, take a few moments to make a toast to the happy times that you have shared thus far with your child(ren). _____

_____
_____
_____
_____
_____
_____
_____
_____
_____
_____
_____
_____
_____
_____
_____
_____
_____
_____
_____
_____
_____
_____
_____
_____

REFLECTION JOURNAL

REFLECTION JOURNAL

Part V
Tips for Communication and Support

Communicating with Your Child

☐ Begin early—while your child is very young—teaching him/her about the people and things you consider "big bad wolves".

☐ Confront and evict "big bad wolves" from your child's life at the onset, and don't hesitate to tell your child about your decision.

☐ Instill in your child a strong sense of God, family, tradition, and culture.

☐ Base your parenting on a specific set of solid core values (seek advice from your church/place of worship).

☐ Establish clear expectations for parent/child communication with your child.

☐ Use every moment as a "teachable moment".

☐ Speak to your child everyday—during the morning and evening.

☐ Enjoy one to two meals and/or snacks with your child each day.

☐ Surprise your child with special gifts, notes, etc. so that he/she knows you love him/her.

☐ Frequently hug, kiss, and tell your child you love him/her—even though he/she may feel he/she is too old for your public displays of affection.

☐ Stand firm in your decisions and compromise when necessary—without throwing away your principles.

☐ Dedicate specific songs to your child and sing them with him/her often while driving in the car or at home.

A MOTHER'S REFLECTION

Signs That Your Child is Going Astray

☐ He/She speaks about moving in with other adults—especially those who have a parenting style contrary to yours

☐ He/She speaks about running away

☐ He/She prefers to use his/her cell phone and/or e-mail—instead of your house phone—to make and accept calls.

☐ He/She erases his/her computer history

☐ He/She prefers to use the computer when you are not nearby

☐ He/She refuses to open up to you—despite your openness and willingness to compromise

☐ He/She prefers that you be more of a "friend" than a "parent"—even when he/she arrives at the same decision as you

☐ He/She prefers visiting friends to inviting them over—even when your home is clean and you offer to make every effort to make their friends feel welcome

☐ He/She is frequently dissatisfied with the amount of freedom you extend him/her—especially as he/she grows older

☐ He/She tries to justify more "mature" music, videos, pictures, etc

☐ He/She is rarely satisfied with his/her appearance—despite compliments from other adults and peers

Finding Support in Your Spouse

☐ Talk openly with one another.

☐ Agree on how to raise your child and modify as your child develops.

☐ Do not allow your child to come between you and your spouse.

☐ Encourage each other by praising each other's strengths and respecting each other's feelings.

☐ Focus on building and maintaining a healthy, happy marriage everyday—especially during difficult moments of child-rearing.

☐ Frequently reflect on the happy and "not so happy" moments of parenting.

☐ Pray for one another.

☐ Discuss your situation with other parents and share what you learn with each other.

☐ Spend time together parenting and as a married couple.

Finding Support in Others

☐ Surround yourself with other like-minded parents, listen to their experiences, and seek advice.

☐ Ask your Church/place of worship to pray for you—especially during difficult moments.

☐ Seek family counseling at the first sign of trouble; issues that may be minor to you—could be major to your child and his/her relationship with you.

☐ Seek support from your child's school (i.e., counselor, teachers, administrators).

☐ Keep your child actively involved in "structured" activities both at school and in the community on a weekly basis.

☐ Consult a variety of print resources from the Internet, library, etc.

☐ Admit that you need help—no matter how great your parenting skills are.

Maintaining Your Sanity

☐ Focus on the positive and give thanks for the opportunity to be a parent—no matter the circumstance.

☐ Read your Bible and pray everyday.

☐ Take time for yourself so that you won't become consumed by your moments of difficult parenting.

☐ Work to make your "house" a "home".

☐ Turn to your spouse for comfort.

☐ Be a role model and hero to your child.

☐ Be patient and tackle one issue at a time.

☐ Give much thought to your reaction/response to each matter and know that ***God always knows how much you can handle***.

☐ Support other parents by helping to keep their families together—any way possible.

Individuals, Families, Schools, Youth Organizations, Parent Groups, Family Service Providers, Churches, and Book Clubs are encouraged to contact the author to arrange for a more in-depth presentation of the contents within this book.

Carletta D. Washington, Ed.S.

education4all@hotmail.com

www.educationfourall.com

(p) 314-438-8440; (f) 314-438-8432

****

Other books by author

Education Reform: The Role and Responsibility of Schools, Parents, Students, and Communities (2006)

Breinigsville, PA USA
30 April 2010
237152BV00001B/5/P